Carving Pen Figures

Steve Brown

Schiffer Publishing Ltd

4880 Lower Valley Rd. Atglen, PA 19310 USA

Dedication

To everyone who purchases this book, Thank you.

Table of Contents

Designed by Laurie A. Smucker
Typeset in Times New Roman/Humanst521 BT/ Americana

ISBN: 0-7643-0609-X
Printed in China

Published by Schiffer Publishing Ltd.
4880 Lower Valley Road
Atglen, PA 19310
Phone: (610) 593-1777; Fax: (610) 593-2002
E-mail: Schifferbk@aol.com
Please write for a free catalog.
This book may be purchased from the publisher.
Please include $3.95 for shipping.

In Europe Schiffer books are distributed by
Bushwood Books
6 Marksbury Avenue
Kew Gardens
Surrey TW9 4JF England
Phone: 44 (0) 181 392-8585; Fax: 44 (0) 181 392-9876
E-mail: Bushwd@aol.com

Please try your bookstore first.

We are interested in hearing from authors with book ideas on related subjects.

Introduction

I was fourteen years old and had worked in a Kentucky coal mine with my Dad since the age of six. You must understand that years ago coal companies allowed this for a few reasons. One, they could work young boys for half the daily wages of $2, and they could send you into the tighter areas of the mine. Why did my Dad allow me to do this? We needed the $3 per day.

When the mines shut down, my Dad took a job driving a truck and I finally went to school for the first time. Yes, a fourteen year old in the first grade and the first from my family to attend school. Not knowing how to read or write, my family had no reason to have ink pens and the like. As I was walking to school on my first day, feeling out of place and not having any school supplies, I came upon a crushed ink pen lying on the side of the road. I picked it up and found that the ink refill was still in good shape. That afternoon I took a small piece of wood, hand drilled a hole in it, then put the refill up into the hole. I then used my worn out Case XX knife and whittled out a miniature baseball bat. This was my very first pen!

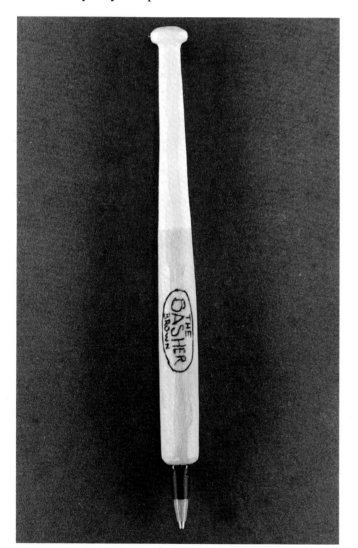

The next day at school my teacher noticed the pen and commented on the unique idea. A few weeks later my teacher was visiting relatives in Louisville and mentioned my pen to her brother who worked for a baseball bat manufacturer. The bat manufacturer got in touch with my family and gave us four round-trip tickets to New York to see the Yankees play. This was in return for the use of the baseball bat pen idea. We had seats in the right field section where Roger Maris hit a home run and Mom caught the ball with her purse. After the game a fellow representing the Yankees offered us $6,100 for the baseball. Come to find out, it was Maris's 61st home run.

So, you ask, what did Mom do with the money we received for selling the baseball? Well, she and an old, white-haired fellow that lived down the road from us went into the restaurant business in Kentucky frying chickens. And you know the rest!

Wow, what a story! And that's exactly what it is. A story that was written with a carved pen!

Buying Pens

All of the pens were carved from the Carve a Pen Kit, available from:

Wood Carvers Supply, P.O. Box 7500, Englewood, Florida 34295;

Woodcraft, 210 Wood County Industrial Park, Parkersburg, West Virginia 26102;

Smoky Mountain Woodcarver's Supply, P.O. Box 82, Hwy. 321, Townsend, Tennessee 37882; or from

Steve Brown, 1805 Forest Acres Drive, Madisonville, Kentucky 42431.

Tool Tips

The following tools were used on all the projects and gallery pieces:

Palm chisels: 1/4-inch, 1/8-inch, 1/16-inch V-tool
#1 veiner
#11 veiner
Fixed-blade carving knife
Leather strop
Cut resistant carving glove

When sharpening, you should wet your stone with mineral spirits or paint thinner in order to keep metal that's removed from your tool from embedding in your stone. This will keep the metal floating while you're sharpening. Keep your stone wet at all times and, when you are finished, just wipe the stone dry. The knife is by far the easiest to sharpen. If your knife is new, start by using a coarse stone. Place one side of the knife flat against the stone. Begin pushing and pulling without lifting the knife. Try and keep up with the amount of strokes. Now flip the knife to the other side and repeat the same number of strokes. When a fine wire edge forms on the cutting edge, switch to a fine stone and repeat using half as many strokes. To remove the wire edge, place the knife flat on your leather strop, cutting edge facing away from you, then pull the knife until that side looks buffed. Now flip the knife and push the knife away from you. Continue buffing until wire edge disappears.

In sharpening a gouge, use only a pulling stroke. Place one tip of the gouge on the stone holding it at a shallow angle. As you pull the gouge, rotate the edge to the opposite tip. After a few pulls over the stone, look at the angle to see if that is the angle you desire. Check this every few strokes. Continue the steps until the fine wire edge appears. Move to the fine stone and repeat these steps. Now pull your gouge over the leather strop. You may want to make a strop that will fit down into the gouge to buff that area. Continue buffing the gouge on the strop until the wire edge disappears.

The same pull strokes are used in sharpening the V-tool. If you are sharpening small V-tools, use only the fine stone. Place one side of the V-tool against the stone holding it at a shallow angle. Pull the tool a few strokes then check for desired angle. Continue strokes until the wire edge forms. Now move to the opposite side and repeat strokes. Always beware of the bottom of the v-tool, the area where the two sides meet, and don't take anymore metal away here than the edges. When the wire edge appears, place the bottom of the v-tool on the stone at the same angle. Pull and rotate this very small area only a few times, then check angle. Now pull the v-tool over the leather strop using the same strokes as with the stone. You may want to make a leather strop with a wedge shape to buff down in the v-tool. Continue to strop all edges until the wire edge disappears. If you have a buffing wheel, this will speed up the process and take the place of the leather strop.

Painting the Pens

All of the pen figures were painted with pre-mixed, acrylic hobby paint thinned to a stain consistency. The pens were then sprayed with a clear matte finish to protect and seal the carvings. After the finish dried, an acrylic antiquing formula was brushed on. A damp rag was used to remove the antiquing.

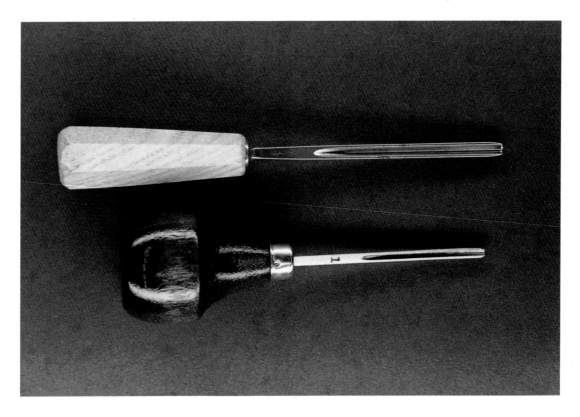

Veiners used: #1 and #11

4

V-tools used: 1/16, 1/8, and 1/4 inch

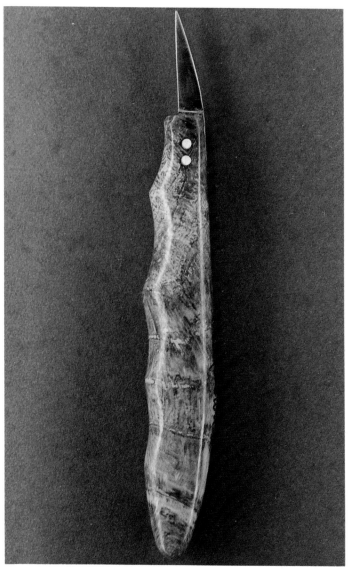

Fixed blade carving knife

5

Chapter 1

Carving the Santa Head

Before carving on any pen kit, insert the ink refill into the wood and trace around the refill where it rests against the wood.

The sideview of the first cut showing the sweeping cut and approximate depth of the cut.

All of the faces I carve, are carved on the corners, not on the flats. Begin by coming down from the top of the pen kit 3/4-inch. This will be the tip of the nose. Here make a sweeping cut back towards the top with your knife.

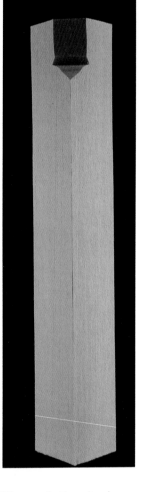

Take your knife and make a V-cut across your first sweeping cut. The V-cut will be placed on the arc of the first sweeping cut. This cut will eventually be part of the eye location.

The location of your V-cut will determine how long or short the nose will be. The further down the arc, the shorter the nose.

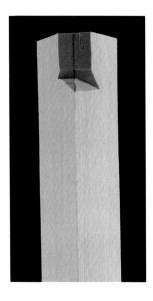

To help keep things equal, pencil in a center line before making the next cuts. Place the side of your knife against the top part of the V-cut. While holding the knife at an angle, push down making a stop cut that does not cut through the center line. Now place your knife at the tip of the nose and push up towards the stop cut following the center line.

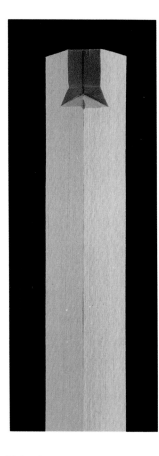

Make the same cuts on the opposite side creating the planes where the eyes will be placed.

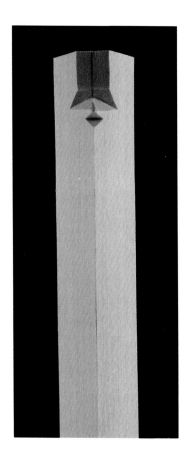

A sideview shows the angle cut to form the lower portion of the nose.

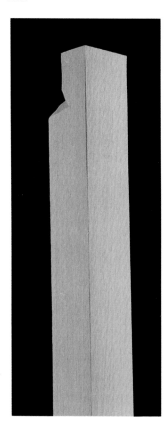

Here you see the angles produced by the cuts.

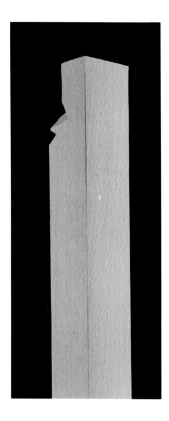

Make a V-cut under the tip of the nose with your knife.

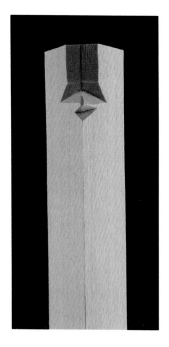

In the next few cuts, you are carving the area where the nostrils will be located. Cut a slight angle; do not cut straight back. This cut will angle up toward the corner of the eye location.

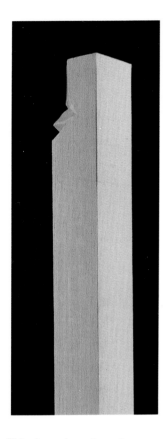

This photo shows how the cut angles toward the eye location.

The #1 veiner is used in the cuts. Place the veiner just to either side of the nose center line and push up and in towards the eye. Take your knife and smooth out the veiner cut. These cuts are producing the bridge of nose and cheek area.

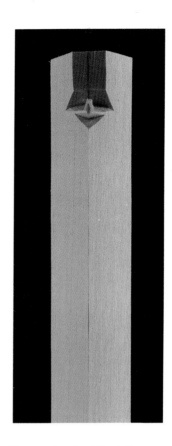

Your carving should look like this after smoothing out both veiner cuts.

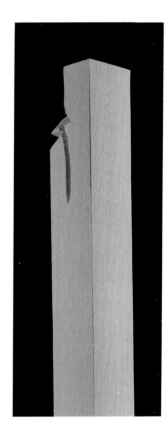

This photo shows the smile or frown line and how it stops at the nose area, creating the back portion of the nostril.

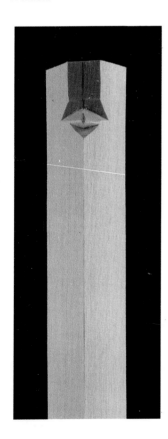

Make the same cuts for the opposite side of the nose.

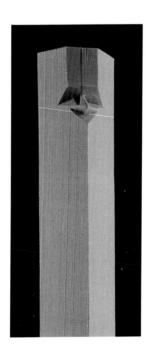

The wood has been turned to give you a better view of the veiner cut.

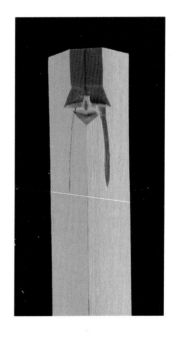

These next cuts will be referred to as the smile or frown lines. Pencil in lines from where the back of nostrils are located. The lines may be as long or short as you wish. Now take your 1/8-inch V-tool and cut along your line.

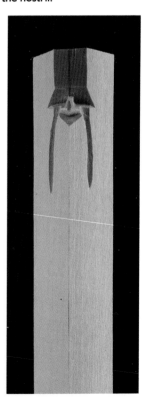

Both smile/frown lines have been cut.

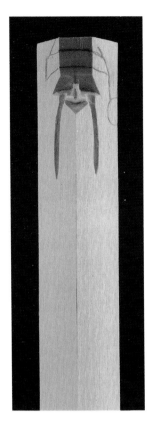

Using the Santa Head pattern, pencil in the Santa cap.

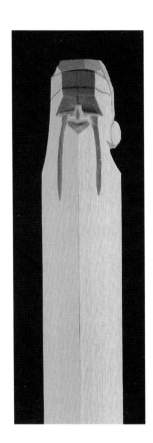

With your knife, remove the wood from the sides of the cap, from top of the cap, and from around the pom-pom.

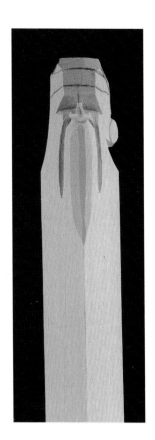

Round the wood from between the smile/frown lines. This is the area where the mustache will be located.

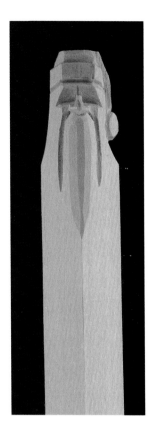

Using your 1/4-inch V-tool and lay out the cap following the lines penciled in.

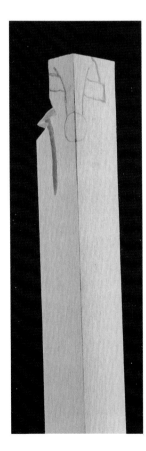

Pencil in sideview of Santa cap.

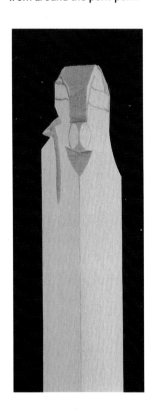

Wood has been removed from back of cap, from top and bottom of pom-pom, and from top of cap.

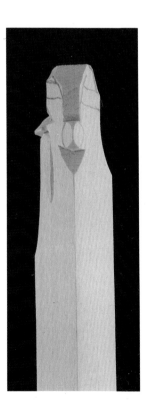

Wood has been removed from under the nose and between smile/frown lines.

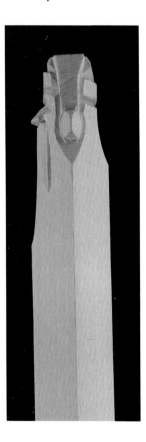

The 1/4-inch V-tool was used to lay out the cap and pom-pom.

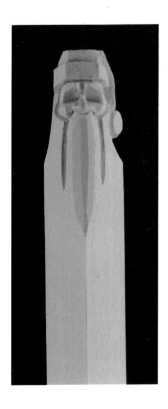

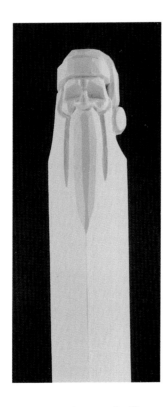

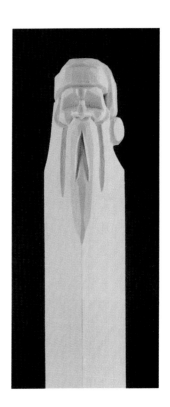

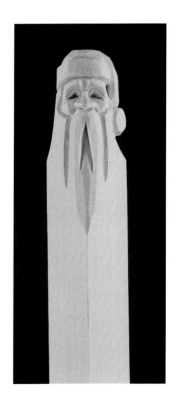

Two different cuts were made in this view. Take your #11 veiner and push up between the eye location making the eye brow. Next take your 1/8-inch V-tool and cut the area where the beard meets the cheek. This cut will continue up to the cap.

Using the knife, smooth off the corners left by the V-tool in forming the cap.

Divide your mustache by taking the tip of your knife and making a deep cut like the one shown. Also, use the tip of the knife to make two shallow cuts under the nose, creating the nostrils.

Since these are very small carvings, eyes are not that difficult to carve. Take the tip of the knife and make two push cuts. One angled up, the other angled down, to form the shape of the eye. This is similar to one that you would put into a Halloween pumpkin. Lay your knife at the cheek area and undercut up to the two push cuts. The triangle piece of wood should pop out, making the eye. Now with the 1/16-inch V-tool, make a cut just above the triangle eye. This will make the eyelid. Using the 1/16-inch V-tool, make a few small cuts on the cheek and outside the corner of the eyes to form small wrinkles.

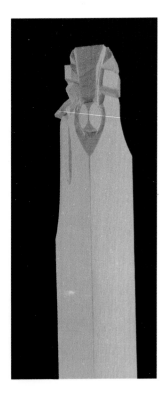

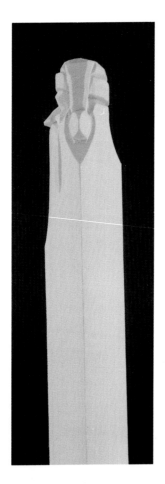

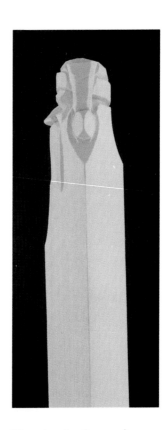

View showing where beard meets cheek area.

The corners have been smoothed on the cap.

View showing the wood removed from mustache.

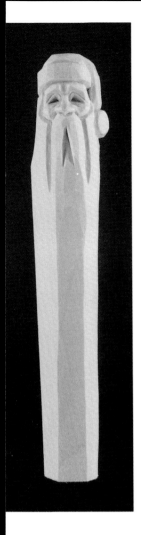

Start removing wood from the corners, tapering the wood down to where the ink refill will be placed.

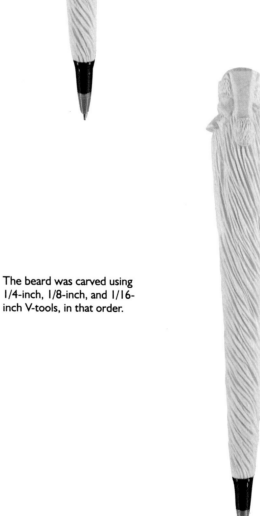

The 1/16-inch V-tool was used to cut the fur on the cap and the pom-pom. This is done by just pricking the wood with the V-tool.

Pencil in the flow of the beard.

The beard was carved using 1/4-inch, 1/8-inch, and 1/16-inch V-tools, in that order.

Insert ink refill.

The carving has been tapered. Round corners on the pom-pom.

Chapter 2

Carving the Wizard

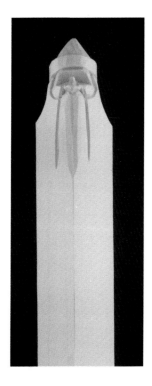

To get to this point in the carving, use the same steps as in the Santa Head chapter.

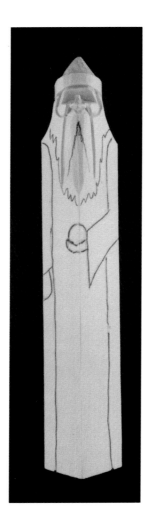

Using the pattern, lay out the design on your wood.

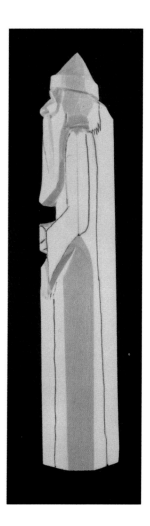

Lay out the sideview on your wood.

All the steps are the same as the Santa Head except the pom-pom is missing.

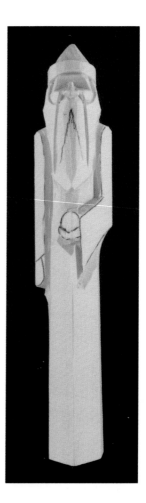

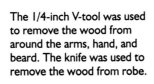

The 1/4-inch V-tool was used to remove the wood from around the arms, hand, and beard. The knife was used to remove the wood from robe.

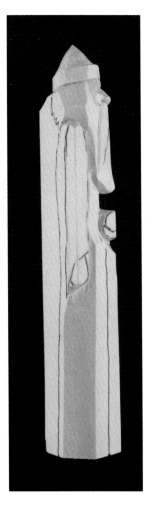

More wood has been removed from robe.

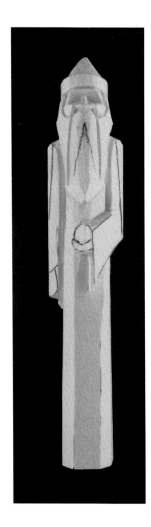

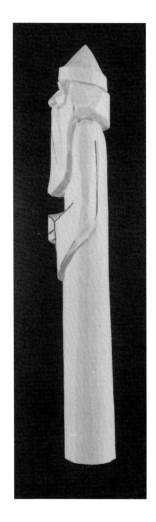

Opposite sideview of the Wizard

Shoulders and robe are more rounded.

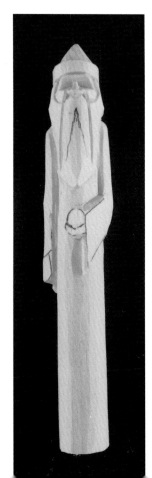

Excess wood can be removed with the knife.

The shoulder width has been reduced and the robe rounded.

13

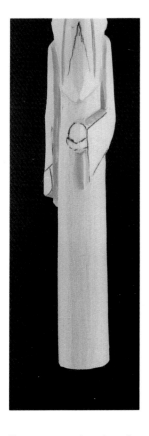

Continue rounding the robe.

More rounding of the arms, shoulders, robe, and crystal ball.

Long wrinkles in the robe are carved with #11 veiner, then tapered with knife.

Eyes have been carved. You may do this step at the beginning. Sometimes I wait to see what I carve in the body to help me judge what size eyes to carve.

Using the knife and 1/8-inch V-tool round up the arms. Cut in the crystal ball and hands. The hands have four planes. The mustache was divided with a knife.

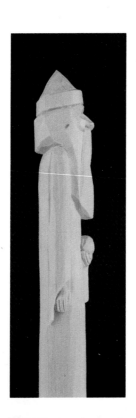

Right sideview showing hand which was carved with the knife and 1/8-inch V-tool. Fingers were cut in with 1/16-inch V-tool.

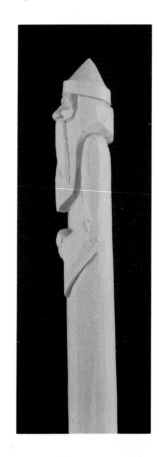

View showing wrinkles of robe.

The 1/16-inch V-tool has been used to carve the beard and hair.

14

Chapter 3

Carving the Nascar Driver

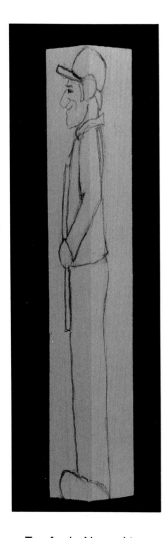

Transfer the Nascar driver pattern to your wood.

Remove the wood from the sideview of the pattern with the knife.

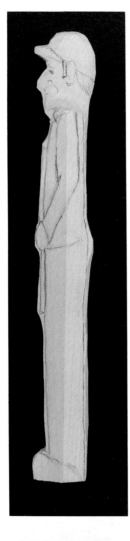

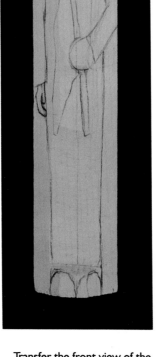

Transfer the front view of the Nascar driver to your wood. Remove the wood from shoulders up to the cap.

With the knife, remove the wood from the driver's sides and around the chin area.

The 1/4-inch V-tool was used to outline the arms.

Using the 1/4-inch V-tool, remove the wood from around the arms. Outline the hands and flag.

With the knife, put the corner shape back on the face area. Cut the V-cut for eye area and V-cut under the nose. The knife was used to undercut the bottom portion of flag.

Back view of Nascar driver showing cuts around arms, hat, and hair.

The angles of the eyes and nose have been carved.

Round the hat, arms, legs, and back areas with the knife. Pencil in the ear and hair. Cut around the area where the pants meet the shoes.

With the 1/8-inch V-tool, carve in the hair outline, the ear, sideburns, and neck area.

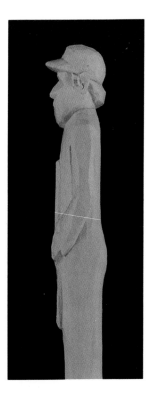

Angles of the eyes and nose shown from the side. The inside of the ear is carved with the tip of the knife.

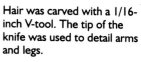

Hair was carved with a 1/16-inch V-tool. The tip of the knife was used to detail arms and legs.

The veiner steps explained in the first chapter have been used around the nose and between the eyes. The smile/frown lines are penciled in.

The triangle cuts for the eyes are made, the nostrils are carved, smile/frown lines are put in with the tip of the knife or 1/16-inch V-tool. The lips are made with the knife.

Here I have used the tip of the knife to highlight around the arms, between the legs, around the flag and the collar. The 1/16-inch V-tool was used to carve in the fingers. Shoes were rounded with the knife.

Sideview of veiner cuts and smile/frown lines.

The profile view of the nose and lip cuts.

The 1/16-inch V-tool is used to carve hair and fingers. The tip of the knife was used to highlight around the flag and neck area.

17

Chapter 4

Carving the Baseball Player

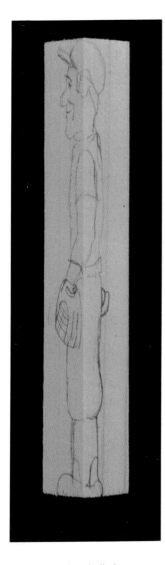

Transfer the front view
pattern to the wood.

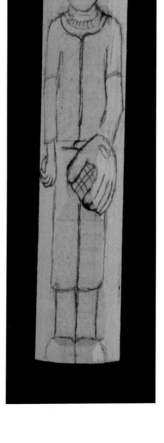

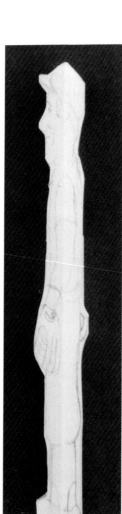

Transfer the baseball player
pattern to the wood.

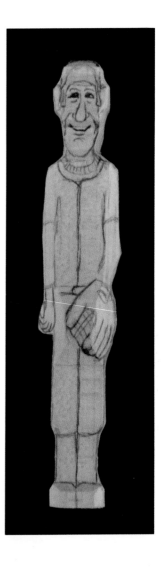

Remove the wood with your
knife from the corners up to
the pattern.

With your knife, remove the
wood from the corners up to
the pattern.

Using the 1/4-inch V-tool, outline the arms, hands, and around the glove.

The knife is used in this step to round the arms, shoulders, legs, and neck.

Reapply the face patterns to your wood.

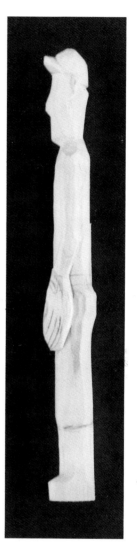

Pencil in the belt line and bottom of pants. Outline cap and ear area with 1/8-inch V-tool.

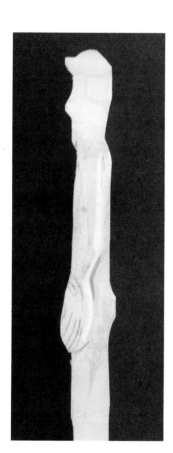

Again the 1/4-inch V-tool was used to remove the wood from around the arms and glove.

Sideview of where the wood was removed from arms, shoulders, legs, and neck.

With your knife, form another corner in the face area. Here you will begin the face steps.

The 1/8 inch V-tool is used to carve cap and ear area. Pencil the pattern for the belt and pants. This view also shows the ball in the right hand.

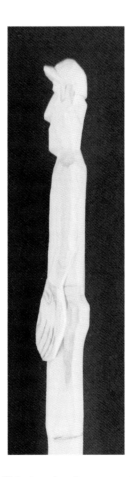

This view showing nose and eye angles.

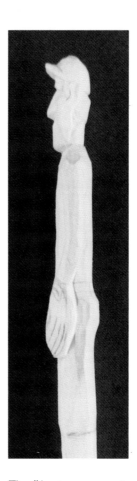

The #1 veiner was used from below the ear down to the jaw area, then the knife was used to blend the jaw and neck area.

The tip of the knife was used to undercut glove, inside ear, around right hand, and the ball. The 1/8-inch V-tool was used around the shirt sleeve.

Cut the eye and nose angles.

Here the veiner has been used on either side of the nose. The 1/8-inch V-tool was used around the neck.

The smile and frown lines are carved, the lips have been carved with the knife, the nostrils cut in with the knife. The tip of the knife was used to round up arms and hand. The 1/8-inch V-tool was used around shirt, neck, and belt area.

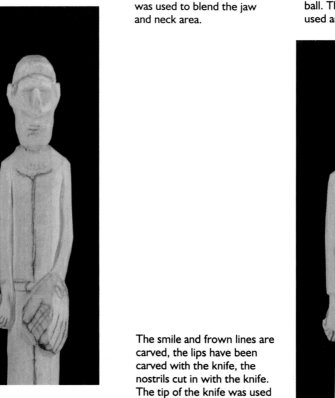

Use the 1/8-inch V-tool to outline the belt, belt loops, around shirt sleeves, and ball. The tip of the knife was used to define the arms.

Define the arms, shirt, and legs with the tip of the knife. Smooth over the glove with the knife, then cut in fingers and pocket of glove with the 1/16-inch V-tool. The 1/16-inch V-tool was also used to cut the shoe soles. Use the #1 veiner to carve the band around the T-shirt. The eyes have been carved and the wrinkles around the eyes.

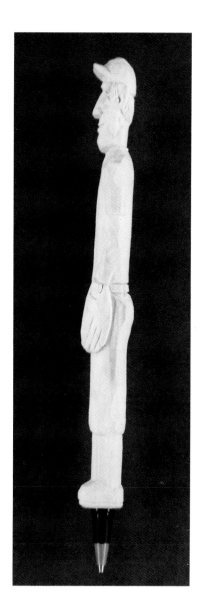

The 1/16-inch V-tool was used to carve the hair. An ink refill is placed into the carving.

Chapter 5

Carving the Golfer

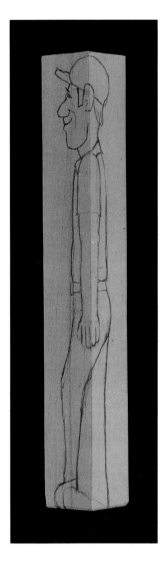

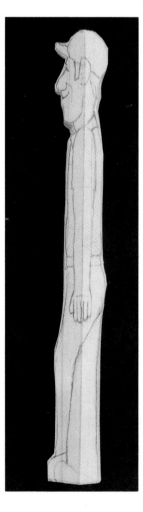

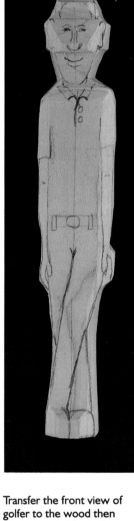

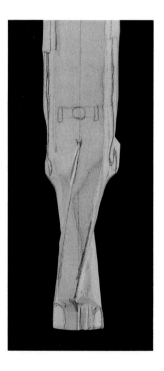

Transfer golfer pattern to the wood.

Remove the wood from corners to pattern.

Transfer the front view of golfer to the wood then remove wood from the corners to the pattern using the knife.

The 1/4-inch V-tool was used to outline legs and shoes.

Using the 1/4-inch V-tool, remove wood from around the right leg and between legs.

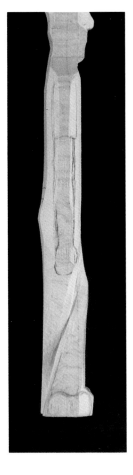

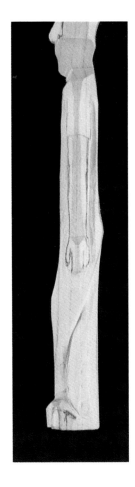

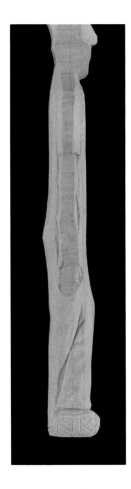

Right side of golfer where 1/4-inch V-tool was used for legs and around shoe.

Sideview of where 1/4-inch V-tool was used to outline arms.

Right sideview showing the rounding of body and left shoe sole. The shoe sole was carved with the 1/16-inch V-tool.

The 1/16-inch V-tool is used to outline belt. Define arms and hands using the knife tip and 1/4-inch V-tool. Make sure you undercut left hand so the golf club will slip up into the hand.

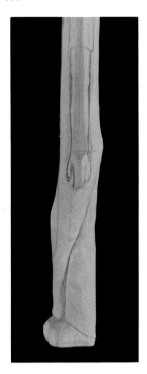

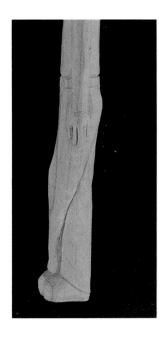

Wood was removed from around lower portion of chin, and the arms were outlined with the 1/4-inch V-tool.

Round the legs, main body, and shoes with knife. Cut a shallow angle on the left shoe. Use the 1/16-inch V-tool to carve the shoe soles.

Left sideview showing the rounding of legs and shoes.

Sideview showing detail of belt and hand, carved with 1/16-inch V-tool.

At this point, all of the face steps have been applied. Use the 1/8-inch and 1/4-inch V-tool to round up the cap and around the ears.

Cut a length of 1/16 inch dowel rod that will reach from the golfer's hand down to his shoe.

After making the V-cut for the grip, use the knife and reduce the diameter of the dowel which will become the shaft of the club.

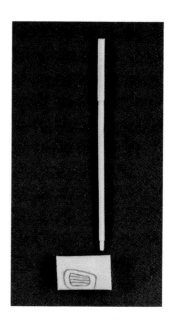

On a 1/8-inch thick piece of scrap wood, lay out the club-head.

Knife tip is used to detail around ear, sideburns, and cap.

For the grip of the golf club, measure down about one third the length of the dowel at this point make a shallow V-cut

At the club-head end of the dowel, measure back 1/16 inch. Then reduce the diameter of dowel at this point. This end will be glued into club-head.

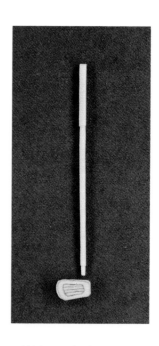

With your knife, carve out the club-head.

Drill a hole in the club head that will fit the end of the dowel.

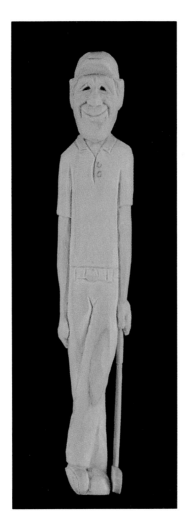

Collar detail was carved with 1/16-inch V-tool. Eyes and lips have been carved.

Now glue the dowel into the club head.

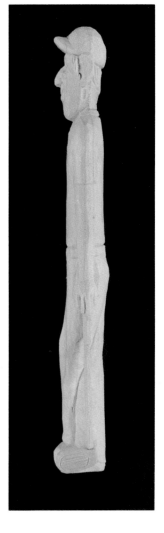

Club, face, and hair are carved with the 1/16-inch V-tool.

Chapter 6

Painting a Pen Figure

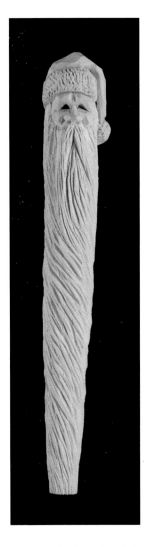

Apply a thinned maroon color paint to the cap. I like using this color for Santas. It is a deep, rich color.

Use pre-mixed acrylic paint and thin your paint to a stain consistency. Here I have applied white to the beard.

In order to give contrast between the white beard and the white on the fur, I have used the paint straight from the container. I did not thin the paint.

Side view.

Side view

You may also use the thinned paint, but put additional coats on the fur to give it contrast.

Medium flesh is used for the face. You may thin paint or use straight from container.

Side view.

To give the Santa rosy cheeks, dip your brush in the thinned maroon paint, then wipe your brush dry. Rub your brush on the cheeks and nose leaving them with a blush. If you did not get enough blush, just apply more in the same manner. If you think you have too much, just wipe it off with a damp rag.

The eyebrows have been painted using the paint straight from the container. Even though you can't see it, a clear matte finish was sprayed on the figure.

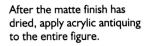

After the matte finish has dried, apply acrylic antiquing to the entire figure.

With a damp rag, wipe away the antiquing leaving the figure as dark or antiqued as you wish. Insert your ink refill and it is ready to use.

27

Gallery and Pen Patterns

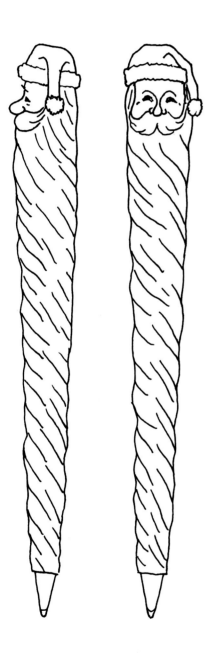

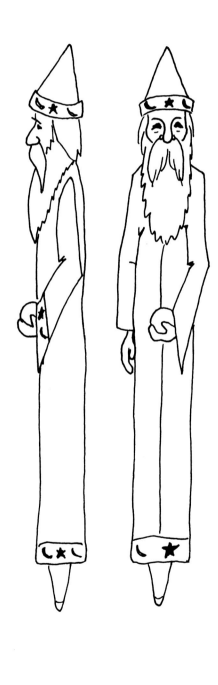

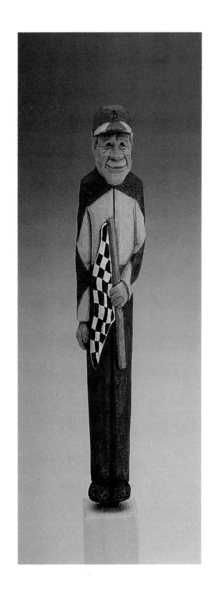

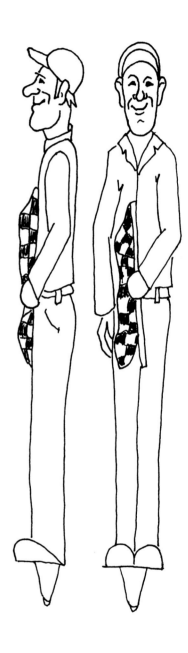

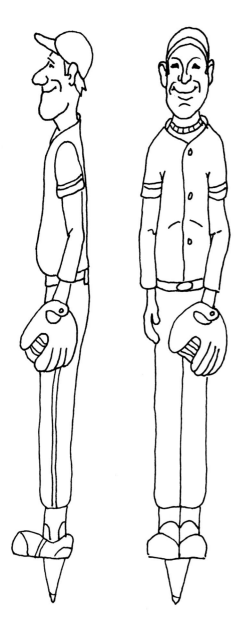

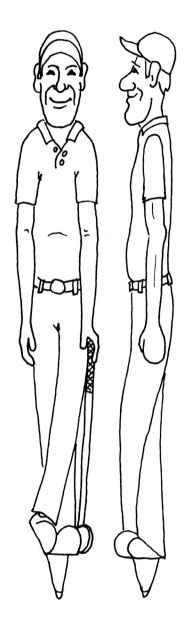

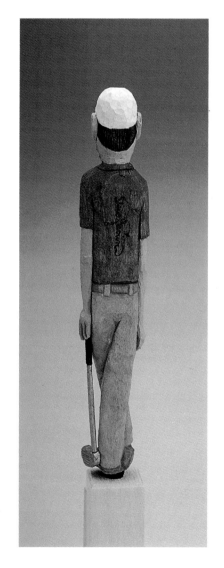

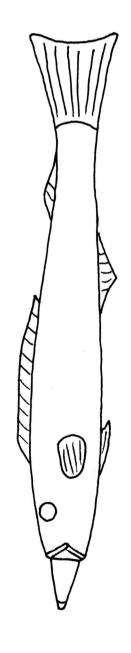

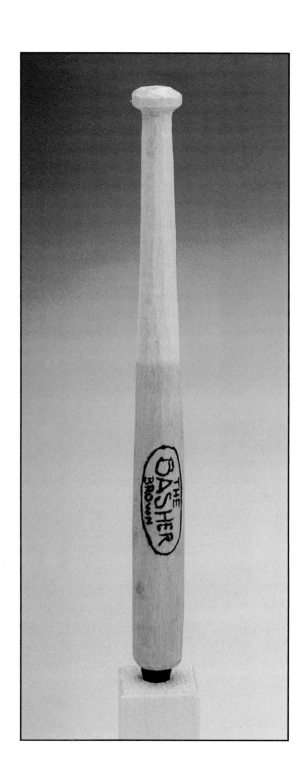

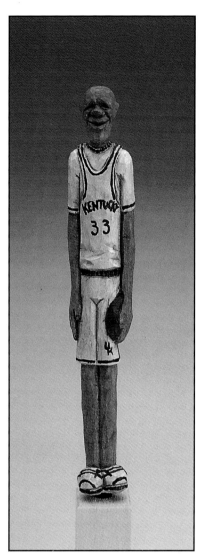

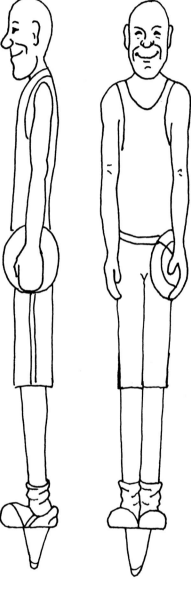

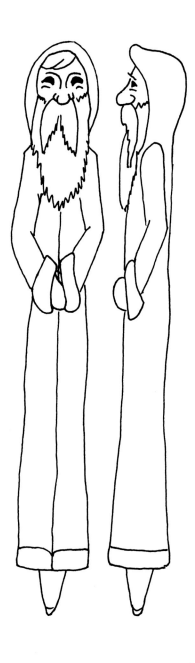

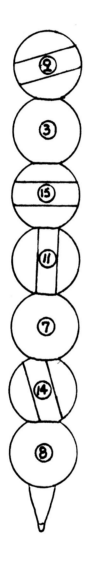

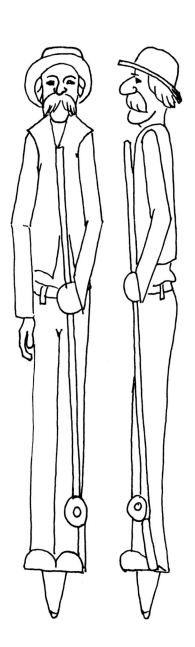

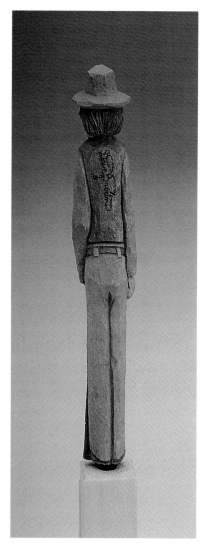

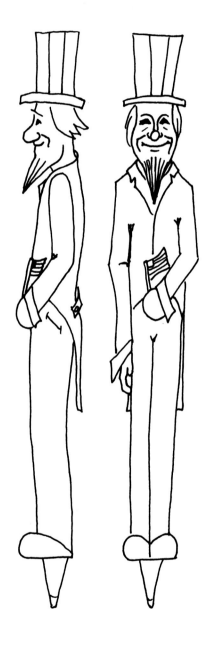

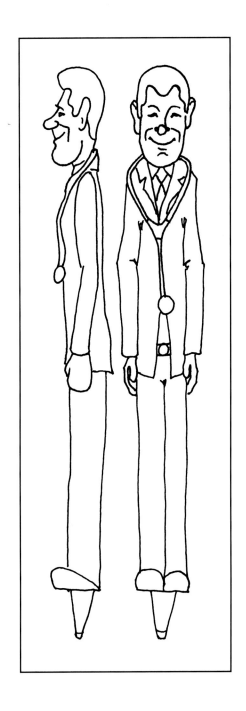

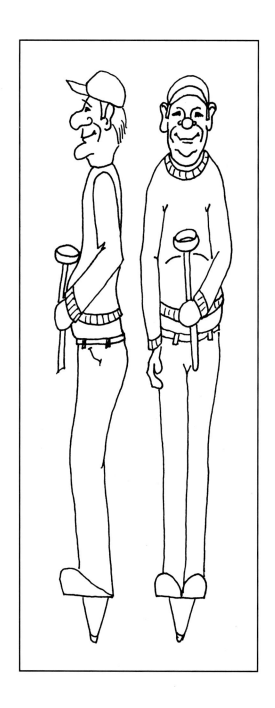

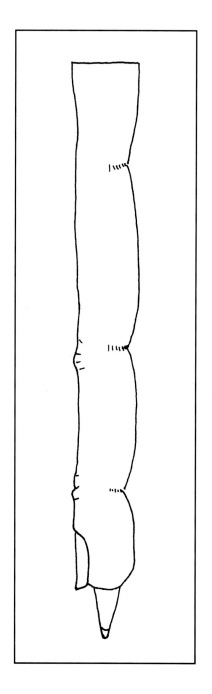

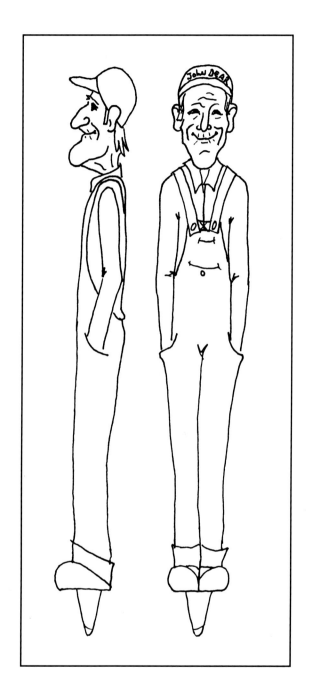

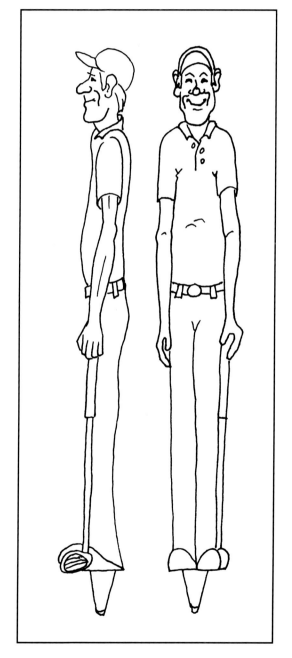

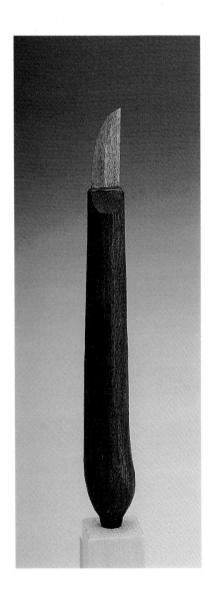

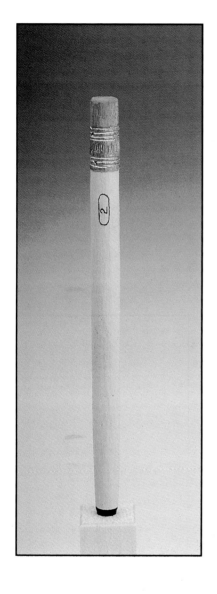

47

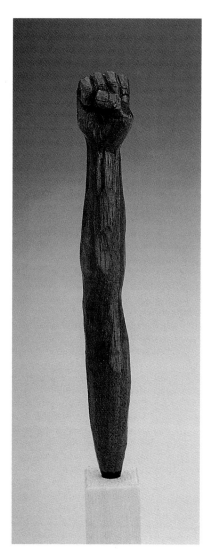